SAN

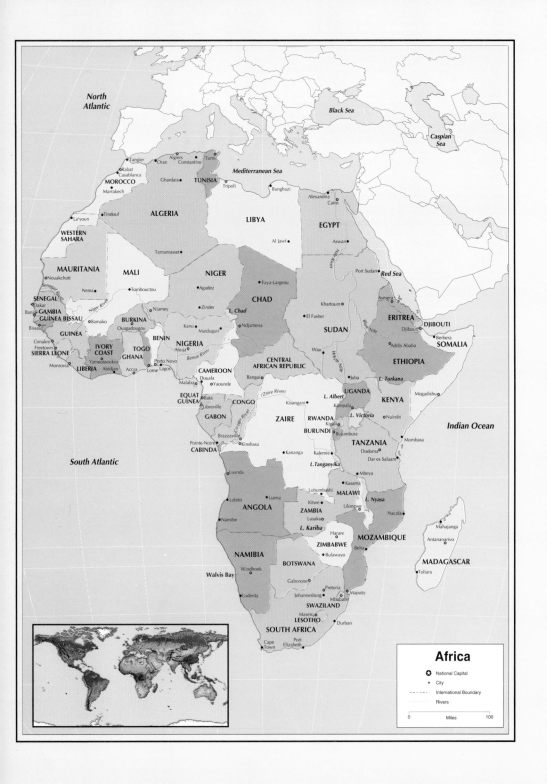

North
Atlantic

Black Sea

Caspian
Sea

Tangier
Oran Algiers Tunis
Constantine

MOROCCO
Rabat
Casablanca
Marrakech
Ghardaia

Mediterranean Sea

Tripoli

Alexandria
Cairo

TUNISIA

Banghazi

La'youn
Tindouf

ALGERIA

LIBYA

EGYPT

WESTERN
SAHARA

Al Jawf

Aswan

MAURITANIA
Nouakchott

MALI

NIGER

Faya-Largeau

Port Sudan Red Sea

Nema

Tombouctou

Agadez

CHAD

Khartoum

Asmera

ERITREA

Senegal River
Dakar
Banjul GAMBIA
GUINEA BISSAU
Bissau

Niger River

Niamey

Zinder

L. Chad

El Fasher

Djibouti DJIBOUTI

Ndjamena

SUDAN

Berbera

Bamako
Ouagadougou

BURKINA

Kano

Maiduguri

SOMALIA

Conakry
Freetown
SIERRA LEONE
Monrovia

GUINEA

BENIN

Wau

Addis Ababa

ETHIOPIA

Porto Novo

Benue River

CENTRAL
AFRICAN REPUBLIC

Bangui

White Nile

Juba

L. Turkana

IVORY
COAST
Yamoussoukro

TOGO
GHANA

NIGERIA
Abuja

LIBERIA

Abidjan

Accra
Lome Lagos

CAMEROON

Douala

UGANDA

EQUAT
GUINEA
Bata

Malabo

Yaounde

(Zaire River)

Kisangani

L. Albert

Kampala

KENYA

Mogadishu

Libreville

CONGO

GABON

ZAIRE

RWANDA
Kigali

L. Victoria

Nairobi

Indian Ocean

Congo River

BURUNDI

Brazzaville

Pointe-Noire
CABINDA
Kinshasa

Kananga

Bujumbura

TANZANIA
Dodoma

Mombasa

South Atlantic

Kalemie

Dar es Salaam

L.Tanganyika

Mbeya

Luanda

Kasama

Lobito
Luena

Lubumbashi

Kitwe

MALAWI

L. Nyasa

ANGOLA
Namibe

ZAMBIA
Lusaka

Lilongwe

Nacala

Mahajanga

Antananarivo

L. Kariba

Harare

MOZAMBIQUE

ZIMBABWE
Bulawayo

Beira

MADAGASCAR

NAMIBIA

BOTSWANA

Toliara

Walvis Bay

Windhoek

Gaborone

Pretoria

Maputo

Luderitz

Johannesburg
Mbabane

SWAZILAND
Maseru
LESOTHO

Durban

SOUTH AFRICA

Cape
Town

Port
Elizabeth

Africa

✪ National Capital

• City

- - - - International Boundary

——— Rivers

0   Miles   100

The Heritage Library of African Peoples

SAN

Megan Biesele, Ph.D. and
Kxao Royal /O/oo

THE ROSEN PUBLISHING GROUP, INC.
NEW YORK

Published in 1997 by The Rosen Publishing Group, Inc.
29 East 21st Street, New York, NY 10010

First Edition

Manufactured in the United States of America

Library of Congress Cataloging-in-Publication Data

Biesele, Megan.
      San / Megan Biesele and Kxao Royal/O/oo. — 1st ed.
         p.   cm. — (The heritage library of African peoples)
      Includes bibliographical references and index.
      Summary: Surveys the history, culture, and contemporary life of
   the San people of Botswana, Namibia, Zambia, Angola, and South
   Africa.
      ISBN 0-8239-1997-8
      1. San (African people)—History—Juvenile literature.   2. San
   (African people)—Social life and customs—Juvenile literature.
   [1. San (African people)]   I. Royal/O/oo, Kxao.   II. Title.
   III. Series.
   DT1058.S36B54   1996
   306′.089′961—dc20   96-38235
                                                                    CIP
                                                                    AC

Contents

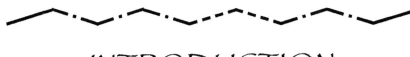

INTRODUCTION

THERE IS EVERY REASON FOR US TO KNOW something about Africa and to understand its past and the way of life of its peoples. Africa is a rich continent that has for centuries provided the world with art, culture, labor, wealth, and natural resources. It has vast mineral deposits, fossil fuels, and commercial crops.

But perhaps most important is the fact that fossil evidence indicates that human beings originated in Africa. The earliest traces of human beings and their tools are almost two million years old. Their descendants have migrated throughout the world. To be human is to be of African descent.

The experiences of the peoples who stayed in Africa are as rich and as diverse as of those who established themselves elsewhere. This series of books describes their environment, their modes of subsistence, their relationships, and their customs and beliefs. The books present the variety of languages, histories, cultures, and religions that are to be found on the African continent. They demonstrate the historical linkages between African peoples and the way contemporary Africa has been affected by European colonial rule.

Africa is large, complex, and diverse. It encompasses an area of more than 11,700,000 square miles. The United States, Europe, and India could fit easily into it. The sheer size is an indication of the continent's great variety in geography, terrain, climate, flora, fauna, peoples, languages, and cultures.

Much of contemporary Africa has been shaped by European colonial rule, industrialization, urbanization, and the demands of a world economic system. For more than seventy years, large regions of Africa were ruled by Great Britain, France, Belgium, Portugal, and Spain. African peoples from various ethnic, linguistic, and cultural backgrounds were brought together to form colonial states.

For decades Africans struggled to gain their independence. It was not until after World War II that the colonial territories became independent African states. Today, almost all of Africa is ruled by Africans. Large numbers of Africans live in modern cities. Rural Africa is also being transformed, and yet its people still engage in many of their customs and beliefs.

Contemporary circumstances and natural events have not always been kind to ordinary Africans. Today, however, new popular social movements and technological innovations pose great promise for future development.

George C. Bond, Ph.D., Director
Institute of African Studies
Columbia University, New York

The San or Bushmen are famous for their traditional lifestyle of hunting and gathering. This San man lives in the Kalahari Desert.

chapter

1

THE PEOPLE

THE TERM SAN REFERS TO A GROUP OF people who speak related Khoisan languages, which contain many click sounds. They live in several countries in southern Africa, including Botswana, Namibia, Angola, Zambia, Zimbabwe, and South Africa.

The most widely known group of San is the hunting and gathering community in the Kalahari Desert.

▼ THE NAME OF THE PEOPLE ▼

The San, also known as Bushmen, are currently debating the name by which they want to be known. They feel that both names, San and Bushman, have been used as negative labels in the past to discriminate against them. Therefore, many of them prefer to be called by the names they use for their individual small groups.

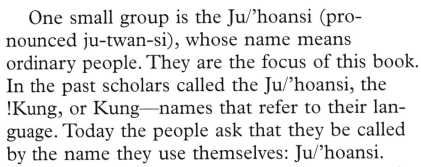

One small group is the Ju/'hoansi (pronounced ju-twan-si), whose name means
ordinary people. They are the focus of this book.
In the past scholars called the Ju/'hoansi, the
!Kung, or Kung—names that refer to their language. Today the people ask that they be called
by the name they use themselves: Ju/'hoansi.

The many small, widely scattered groups of
San have only recently begun to discuss the
issues that they have in common. They have not
yet agreed upon a general term or name to cover
everyone. For the moment we use the general
term San, though the people may soon choose a
different term to describe themselves.

▼ LANGUAGE ▼

The name Ju/'hoansi and many other written
words in the Khoisan (pronounced coy-san)
languages contain unfamiliar symbols. The apos-
trophe in Ju/'hoansi calls for a glottal stop,
which is a break in a word's sound. There are
four (or sometimes five) click consonants in
these languages (see box on page 11).

These and other features of the Khoisan languages distinguish them from all other language
groups of Africa and the world.

The original click languages of Africa are very
ancient, as are the ancestral lines of the people
who now speak them. However, some Bantu
languages of southern Africa, like Xhosa, only

MAKING CLICKS

The "/" is the first click consonant. It is made by drawing the tip of the tongue away from the back of the teeth. This makes a slightly scolding sound, like "tsk, tsk!"

The second click, "=", is made by doing the same thing with the tongue, but from the small ridge just behind the front teeth. This sound is a soft "pop."

The third click, "!", is the strongest sound, like the noise made when removing the tab on a soda can. It is made by pointing the tongue straight up against the roof of the mouth and drawing it down suddenly.

The fourth click, "//", is a clucking sound made on both sides of the mouth simultaneously. It is like the sound one makes to urge on a horse.

Some Khoisan languages have a fifth, or "kiss," click. It sounds like there is a kiss in between the other letters of a word.

Although the clicks are difficult to learn, they are easy to pronounce when learned. A person learning the clicks can substitute a "t" sound for the first two clicks, and a "g" sound for the third and fourth. The "kiss" click is easy for almost anyone to make.

adopted click sounds from the Khoisan languages several centuries ago.

▼ BEYOND THE ROMANTIC VIEW ▼

The traditional lifestyle of the San relies on a specialized knowledge of their natural environment. For example, the San survive in arid areas by gathering nutritious plants and by burying

HISTORY AND DIVERSITY

Learning about San history is the best way to avoid ideas about them that are biased, romantic, simplified, or incorrect.

People who live in modern cities often think that hunters and gatherers like the San lead a life that is peaceful and ideal. In fact, the history of the San in southern Africa has been far from pleasant or easy. Their contact with other peoples has often led to bloodshed. Outsiders were often prejudiced against the San and regarded them as less than human. As a result many San groups lost their land and were forced to become laborers. Others were actually treated like undesirable animals and hunted and killed like vermin. Many San lost their lives in this way.

The San did not accept this situation passively: they fought back. They often formed bandit gangs to raid cattle and sheep belonging to the white and black settlers who encroached upon their hunting grounds.

Outsiders found it hard to accept the San because of their different physical features, their unfamiliar clicking languages, and their special knowledge of the natural environment. Ignorant outsiders who could not understand the San's lifestyle labeled the San as lazy, unambitious, and unable to plan for the future.

Today we understand that such racist stereotypes are wrong. We can appreciate that the San provide us with an example of a lifestyle in which people live in harmony with their environment and strive for harmony among the members of their community.

precious water in ostrich eggshells along their travel routes. They put natural poisons on their hunting arrows and skillfully track their wounded prey for long distances until the animals eventually become drugged and drop.

This lifestyle of hunting and gathering depends on a deep understanding of the natural world. Today many people feel that the modern world has lost touch with nature. Most people's survival now has nothing to do with hunting and gathering wild foods, which was how all early humans lived. The fact that many San still follow this ancient way of life, close to nature, has led many outside observers to form a romantic view of the San. They view them as living ideal and heroic lives.

A romantic view is often based on unrealistic beliefs, not on facts. People with a romantic view of the San fail to see them as fellow members of the modern world who have many of the same desires, goals, and problems as others. Many people prefer to believe that the San—and others who have retained their ancient lifestyles—live in a completely harmonious world. Too often, exactly the opposite is true.

The San, like many of the world's indigenous peoples, today face the loss of their land and livelihood. Like other hunters and gatherers, they have a tradition that land cannot be owned as it is in the Western world. They also tend to step aside when more aggressive peoples try to take their land and resources.

In many cases the San have lost their ancient land, and with it both their familiar natural resources and the right to an independent life. Many San today are becoming politically active in an effort to protect their land and human rights.

San groups are found in several countries of southern Africa. The best-known San are those who live in the Kalahari Desert, which covers parts of Botswana, Namibia, and South Africa.

▼ THE SAN IN SOUTHERN ▼
AFRICAN HISTORY

San peoples have been divided by scholars into five major language families: /Xam, !Kung, Ta'a, !Wi, and Khoe. All San groups fall into one of these families, although the groups seem to have lived for long periods in isolation—even from other small groups who spoke the same language. We know this from measuring both similarities and changes in their languages. From these findings, experts can identify probable migration routes into southern Africa and trace the probable history of the various languages.

Many San today blend their ancient traditions with new ways. Seen here is a traditional healer named /Kunta Boo wearing his hunting gear: a skin bag, a quiver containing his bow and poisoned arrows, and a short spear. For thousands of years the San survived by hunting, but today cattle herding has taken over much of the land where the San live.

Their conclusions are based on the differences between the Khoisan languages spoken today in different areas of the subcontinent.

There are two main subgroups of San peoples—hunters and herders. Before the San hunters came in contact with cattle-owning peoples such as the Xhosa and Tswana, they lived by hunting and gathering, or foraging. These foragers are generally known as the San. After meeting up with herding peoples, some San became herders themselves. They kept cattle and sheep but also foraged at times as well. These herders are known as Khoekhoe (pronounced coy-coy) or Khoi. Today the major Khoekhoe populations are found in South Africa and Namibia.

Taken together—Khoi and San—the names for these peoples produce the term Khoisan. This term is sometimes used to refer to both San and Khoekhoe peoples, who are linked by their similar languages, appearances, and cultural features.

The Khoekhoe herders have long been thought to have ties to eastern and northern Africa. Experts believe that the animals they herd—especially the fat-tailed sheep—were gradually brought over from east and north Africa between 2,000 and 4,500 years ago.

Unlike the herders, it is impossible to pinpoint the origins of the San hunters. For the most part, the oral literature of the San did not include historical accounts. And until recently none of their languages were written down. Today many anthropologists believe that the ancestors of the San once lived all over southern and eastern Africa. Most anthropologists and language experts agree with the San themselves in regarding the San as the aboriginal inhabitants of southern Africa. It seems likely that the San peoples have lived where they are now for thousands of years.▲

chapter

2

THE KALAHARI DESERT

MOST SAN IN NAMIBIA, BOTSWANA, ZAMBIA, Zimbabwe, and South Africa live in or near the Kalahari Desert. The Kalahari spans most of southern Africa from east to west, with its center in Botswana.

▼ LIVELIHOOD ▼

The San's means of making a living varies according to their environments. The Kalahari Desert has a wide variety of mini-environments. To gain the most benefit from these local conditions, different San groups have developed specialized forms of hunting and gathering. For example, in the Okavango Swamps in northern Botswana, the San survive by fishing, hunting, and gathering.

Today some San keep cattle, goats, and sheep while others work for wages. Because of changing political and economic circumstances, San

If a sufficient amount of rain falls, the Kalahari Desert turns green for about three months of the year. The top picture shows a natural pool in Namibia. The middle picture shows the rainy season in Botswana. The bottom picture shows an enormous baobab tree in Namibia during the dry season.

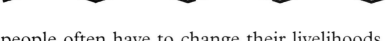

people often have to change their livelihoods several times during their lifetimes.

▼ THE KALAHARI ▼

Until about 10,000 years ago, all human societies lived by hunting and gathering. Information about the Kalahari foragers can help us understand the past of human society. However, the Kalahari has many different environments within its vast borders. We must therefore guard against generalizing too much about the past from what we know of the San economies today.

Before colonization, San peoples lived in small, widely scattered groups. The sizes of their groups varied according to the environment's natural resources.

Their foods included many kinds of large antelopes, small animals, and a wide selection of tree fruits, nuts, berries, underground tubers (root vegetables like potatoes), and the *tsama* melon (the ancestor of our watermelon).

▼ JU/'HOANSI DIET ▼

For the past 40,000 years the Ju/'hoansi have maintained a healthy diet using very simple techniques, such as hunting with bows and arrows and carrying water in ostrich eggshells. Today older people still have a great deal of specialized knowledge about their territory and the more than one hundred plant foods and fifty-five animal species on which they have based their food supply. Their staple food is a highly nutritious nut called the *mongongo*. *Mongongo* trees grow along sand dunes in the Ju/'hoansi area. The purple fruit around the nut is boiled off and made into an edible porridge. Then the delicious nut is roasted.

The diet of the Ju/'hoansi, like that of other San groups, is thus based on what their specific environment has to offer. In the Central Kalahari Reserve, located in the middle of Botswana, there is no year-round staple food like the *mongongo*. Instead the G/wi and other San peoples there use up to thirteen main foods in the course of a year.

The lives of the San are changing rapidly as many become involved in the modern economies and the politics of the countries where they live. However, many Ju/'hoansi today still

The *mongongo* nut is the basis of the Ju/'hoansi diet. Here the fruit is shown life size and cut in half to see the nut.

Ju/'hoansi teenagers play an important part in San society. This boy climbs up pegs knocked into a baobab tree. The pegs make it easy to harvest honey from a beehive in the tree at any time.

survive by collecting vegetable foods that ripen at different times of the year. These plants, which provide 80 percent of their diet, were traditionally gathered by women. Because of this work, women had equal status with men in making decisions.

Men hunted animals as large as giraffes and as small as mice to provide animal protein in the diet. Sometimes women helped their husbands track animals. San hunting depends on specialized knowledge of animal behavior, extraordinary tracking skills, and the use of lightweight, poison-tipped arrows. Today, because larger

game is increasingly rare, mainly smaller animals are hunted.

▼ LEISURE ▼

Contrary to popular belief, hunting and gathering in a semidesert environment is not a risky or unreliable form of existence. Using a thorough knowledge of their environment, hunter-gatherers can survive even difficult periods relatively easily. Though this lifestyle can be strenuous at times, the people also have plenty of leisure time.

Ju/'hoansi adults can provide enough food for the whole group by working an average of only two to three days per week. Because they satisfied their needs so easily and worked so little, the Ju/'hoansi and the other San foragers of southern Africa have been called "the original affluent society." But they were affluent only when they were able to control their environment and lifestyle. As soon as outsiders interfered, San people quickly faced poverty.▲

chapter

3

SOCIAL VALUES

THE JU/'HOANSI OF NYAE NYAE, AN AREA OF
nearly 4,000 square miles in northeastern
Namibia, are among the last San groups in
southern Africa who have a lifestyle similar to
the ancient way of life.

▼ SHARING ▼

Today, as in the past, small groups of local
Ju/'hoansi share resources found on the land
using agreed rules. No one group has exclusive
rights to any piece of land. Frequent visiting and
sharing among the different groups reduces and
smooths out local shortages. Groups related by
marriage cooperate. They join together in a
given area when there is sufficient food and
water, but live apart when sources of food and
water are hard to find.

However, there are now some differences in
this ancient pattern. Economic and governmen-
tal pressures encourage permanent settlement,

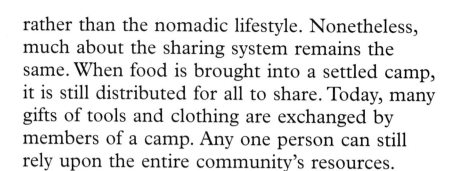

rather than the nomadic lifestyle. Nonetheless, much about the sharing system remains the same. When food is brought into a settled camp, it is still distributed for all to share. Today, many gifts of tools and clothing are exchanged by members of a camp. Any one person can still rely upon the entire community's resources.

▼ PROPERTY ▼

In the past, individuals and groups had to move constantly in order to stay close to their food sources as animals moved and different plant foods ripened. Personal property was minimal, usually weighing less than twenty-five pounds per individual. Shelter, clothing, and tools were made easily, and there was ample leisure time to make them.

This pattern is changing somewhat now that people are becoming settled. However, the San still make do with much less property than most other people.

In the past, frequent moves and the emphasis on sharing made storing food difficult. Also, stored food spoiled quickly in the Kalahari heat. The environment itself was the storehouse for the Ju/'hoansi and the other San. Even today, the San forage only when they need food. They distribute and consume the food as soon as they collect it. Food is eaten fresh. It is not supposed to be hoarded or kept for later use.

Men and women share the responsibility of obtaining food for the group. Men do the hunting (top) and women gather wild foods (below).

Because San groups move about a great deal, their houses are temporary. A shelter such as the one above is made of branches and twigs, sometimes thatched with grass. It takes only a few hours to make.

There is also a remarkable lack of emphasis on wealth and prestige, or status, among the San. No one is supposed to stand out from the rest of the group. If someone comes back from a successful hunt showing excessive pride, he is put firmly in his place—even if the kill is a large animal.

▼ EGALITARIANISM ▼

An egalitarian society is one in which old and young, leaders and ordinary people, and women and men all have equal status. The San's emphasis on sharing equally and their lack of status roles make them one of the most egalitarian societies in the world. Their rules of sharing work well for them because their society is based on living together in small groups of

people who are related and know each other
well.

▼ COMMUNITY LIFE ▼

With this sharing ethic, the San were able to
live together in relative harmony in the past. The
Ju/'hoansi, for example, typically lived in groups
of ten to thirty closely related people. Each
group, called a band, lived in its own camp.

A camp consisted of about six shelters,
arranged in a half- or quarter-circle around an
open area. Shelters were made of woven grass
supported on a framework of sticks. Archa-
eologists have found strong evidence that people
living much like today's Ju/'hoansi made similar
homes in this area as far back as 40,000 years
ago. This suggests that communities have consisted of small camps for a very long time.

In times of plenty these small bands met up
with other bands and spent time together. Six or
seven bands typically existed within a sharing
network.

▼ RECENT CHANGES ▼

Today the Ju/'hoansi, like most San, no longer
live in isolation. They now live side by side with
agricultural peoples like the Tswana and the
Herero. These groups make their living by
keeping herd animals and raising crops such as
corn, melons, and beans. The San now live in

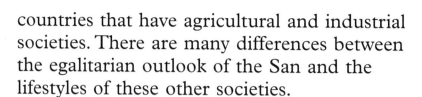

countries that have agricultural and industrial societies. There are many differences between the egalitarian outlook of the San and the lifestyles of these other societies.

Foraging is an immediate way to make a living: time spent hunting or gathering is rewarded almost immediately. In contrast, agriculture requires repetitive, often tiring physical labor that is rewarded later in the year at harvesttime. An industrial society is based on manufacturing goods or providing services. This type of economy finds its reward in monetary profits.

Agricultural and industrial societies generally use a labor force to produce their goods and services. Often the labor is supplied by younger, poorer, or less advantaged people under a system of authority that controls the wealth. For example, a chief may give land and resources to those of lesser rank. The president of a company determines whom to employ and how much to pay them. Thus, these societies are divided into classes or status levels. This is known as social stratification. Societies based on social stratification are the opposite of the egalitarian system used by the San.

Stratified societies store wealth. Farmers usually store it in the form of large herds of animals or crops. Industrial societies store wealth in the form of money. Storage encourages

FOLKLORE AND LEARNING

For the Ju/'hoansi, a key issue is how best to share limited local resources. Folklore, such as the following story, helps teach young people the attitudes and knowledge they need to live well in the Kalahari. The stories do not end with a moral lesson. Instead, they illustrate memorably what happens if people do not live by social rules.

Uhu and his mother were out collecting sweet potatoes. Uhu found a tortoise in the field. Instead of sharing the tortoise with his mother, Uhu roasted the tortoise and ate it alone. His mother was very angry with Uhu for not sharing his food, so she went to look for food elsewhere. When she was out of sight of Uhu, she pulled the ends of her skirt through her legs, rose up into the sky, and disappeared. Uhu went off to find his mother, following her footprints. He came to the place where his mother had stopped but couldn't find any more footprints. "Mother of mine!" he cried. But his mother did not come back. That day, Uhu turned into a bird who lives alone. He still feeds on the tortoises that he denied his mother.

The story suggests that having the treat of roasted tortoise all to yourself is not worth the price of losing your mother and your humanity.

hoarding. The competition between individuals for greater wealth and power easily becomes the basis for these types of societies.

San societies and individuals now face important choices between their traditional way of life and these other systems.▲

chapter

4

COMMUNITY LIFE

THE GREAT EQUALIZER IN THE SOCIAL LIFE
of the Ju/'hoansi is the need to share. Each person knows that by sharing, one is ensuring that others will return the favor when he or she comes home empty-handed.

Ownership for the Ju/'hoansi and other San peoples means more than just collecting and keeping things for oneself; it includes the responsibility of sharing with others. Sharing itself, which minimizes risk, is an important resource in an unreliable environment.

▼ FAMILIES AND BANDS ▼

Nuclear families are the primary units within which gathered foods are shared. However, the goods gathered by one nuclear family are not enough to sustain the hunting and gathering lifestyle. For this reason, families are organized into extended-family bands. These bands have

San communities share important resources such as water. These children playing at a pool are taking part in an education project in a Nyae Nyae village in Namibia.

up to thirty people in them. The size ensures that there will be enough men to hunt and enough women to forage. Foraging and hunting are quite social. The San peoples often talk and play while they are working.

▼ *N!ORE* ▼

A band of related Ju/'hoansi uses the resources of its own *n!ore*. A *n!ore* is an area that provides its small group with enough food and water to live there throughout the seasons.

The San marry into different *n!ores* to create alliances. They often visit each other to share food and resources. Sometimes the rain may be spotty, causing bush foods to sprout or ripen faster in one *n!ore* than in another. People visit their relatives at a lush *n!ore* when they need

31

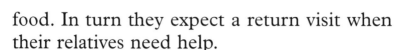

food. In turn they expect a return visit when their relatives need help.

Leadership of *n!ores* is not stratified. Rather, each *n!ore* has stewards, a core group of brothers and sisters who have the responsibility of sharing its resources among the band. Stewards ensure that food is economically gathered to prevent the area from being depleted of plants and animals.

The *n!ore* system is based on well-known kinship rules. There is general agreement about which band has primary rights to which areas. The boundaries of allied bands' lands are not precise. A hunting territory is a somewhat circular area that might, for example, extend south and west of a certain range of hills. Animals within such hunting territories belong to no one until they are shot, and they may be shot even by visiting bands. This flexibility is important in relieving local food shortages in times of brief drought.

In years of severe drought, however, food is scarce everywhere. Then there is no point in visiting an allied band's territory and no reason for conflict.

▼ *KXAOSI* (OWNERS) ▼

One important way that the use of land is shared by the band is through the concept of *kxaosi* (singular: *kxao*), or owners. Owners are really stewards who have expert knowledge of a

hives are important resources for San
ds. In the top picture, the *kxao*, or
er, of a hive has climbed about thirty
up a tall tree to reach the honey.
r stunning the bees by placing a
king branch into the hive, he and his
er remove honey. San women play
lly important roles in gathering wild
ds. They also look after their children.
woman (right) is carrying her baby in
aded skin cloak called a kaross.

San hunters stalk their prey with great skill. They creep very close to the animals before shooting poisoned arrows. The light arrows only need to nick an animal's skin for the poison to enter the bloodstream. Hunters follow the animal until it collapses from the poison.

particular resource. A *g!ukxao*, or owner of water, is an informed person who tends a water source so it can be shared.

The person responsible for killing the animal is its *kxao* and has the right to distribute the meat. The *kxao* might be either the hunter or someone who had loaned an arrow to the hunter. Meat is a vital resource. In the 1950s Ju/'hoansi bands, consisting of about twenty-five people each, killed fifteen to eighteen large mammals per year. Today smaller animals are the main source of meat.

Even those who might never actually hunt, such as women or handicapped people, can loan their arrows to hunters. In this way they can become *kxaosi* of the meat and share it with others. Sharing food at one time entitles them to a share of meat any time that it is available.

Meat is shared with all members of the local groups according to how closely the members are related to the *kxao*. Rules of meat distribution are very complex. For example, certain portions must be reserved for particular relatives and for absent band members. If any of these rules are violated, bad feelings can arise. Meat distribution continues to be a high point of tension among the Ju/'hoansi.

Vegetables and other bush foods are not shared as carefully as meat, although they far outweigh meat in importance in the total diet. The woman who gathers bush foods shares them casually with her nuclear family, then with others if there is enough. What is *not* casual about the bush foods, however, is the ownership of food territories.

Certain bands have primary ownership of specific fruit trees. For example, the band that owns a certain type of fruit tree must be consulted by others prior to taking ripe fruit. This form of ownership keeps the number of users in line with the amount of available food.▲

chapter

5

RELIGION AND HEALING

THE WORLDVIEW OF THE JU/'HOANSI AND other San is closely related to their religious ideas and ceremonial life. Physical and psychological healing are regarded as largely spiritual matters.

▼ GOD ▼

The Ju/'hoansi believe in a great God who created the earth and all that is in it, including death and evil. God has several names, which can only be spoken aloud according to strict rules of respect. The Ju/'hoansi names for God include !Xu, Old G=kao, and Kaoha. !Xu has a wife called Koba, which means mother of the bees.

God's creation includes a supernatural world that parallels our own. It is inhabited by the spirits of human relatives who have died. These relatives remain in contact with the world of the

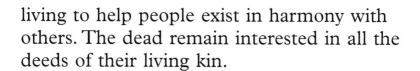

living to help people exist in harmony with others. The dead remain interested in all the deeds of their living kin.

▼ DEITIES ▼

Besides the great God and his wife, there are several lesser gods or deities. One important Ju/'hoansi deity is G//aoan. He lives in the western sky and is the leader of the spirits of the dead. He sends messages and misfortunes to human beings by way of their dead ancestors.

The Ju/'hoansi believe they can communicate directly with their deities and dead relatives through thought, prayer, and dreams. Sometimes, such as when there is very bad thunder and lightning, the Ju/'hoansi scold their gods loudly.

▼ SUPERNATURAL FORCES ▼

Many things that happen to the Ju/'hoansi are attributed to supernatural forces. These forces were created by the great God, !Xu, but after he made them, he allowed the forces to operate on their own. One supernatural force, called *n!ao*, is a power related to animals, weather, and newborn babies.

The most important supernatural force is *n/om*, a magical energy that is found in many forms throughout the universe. It can be developed and used by human beings for what the Ju/'hoansi regard as the most important human

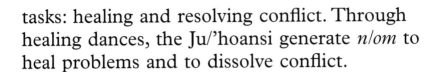

tasks: healing and resolving conflict. Through
healing dances, the Ju/'hoansi generate *n/om* to
heal problems and to dissolve conflict.

▼ DANCING AND HEALING ▼

Living in small bands in a harsh environment
can sometimes cause problems among the
Ju/'hoansi. Although these conditions may cause
some people to become angry with each other,
the Ju/'hoansi's survival depends upon avoiding
conflict with one another. Since the hunting and
gathering groups are so interdependent, conflict
can keep them from having shelter and food.
Basic necessities thus depend on continued good
will, which healing dances create.

Healing dances are the center of the people's
ceremonial life. Sessions have a deep spiritual
meaning. Participating in intense and exhilarat-
ing all-night healing dances generates spiritual
power that heals, protects, and gives well-being
to all. They are a way for the people to meet
their physical, spiritual, and emotional needs
and therefore to stay in harmony.

The healing dance is the main method for
treating illnesses, though the Ju/'hoansi also use
medicinal herbs and salves for minor injuries
and infections and have recently begun to use
antibiotics.

Arguments between villages or disagreements
about sharing meat are problems that are often

Regular healing dances are a vital part of San life. They are generally held at night around a fire but they can be held at any time.

mended in healing dances. If someone's illness takes a serious turn, a dance may be organized. More often, however, there will be a smaller healing ceremony in which one or two healers, with several singers, work exclusively on the sick person. Since healing energy originates from God, both dancing and individual healing are spiritual exercises.

In the healing dance, everyone shares the spiritual power of *n/om*. The Ju/'hoansi say the power is found in the dance fire, in the healing songs, and in the healers most of all. *N/om* concentrates in the pit of the healers' stomachs and the base of their spines. The dance generates the

During healing dances women generally clap and sing while men dance.
However, this is not a rule; both sexes can clap, sing, and dance.

n/om in the healers; their singing and dance
moves "heat up" the *n/om*. When *n/om* boils, it
vaporizes and rises up the spine.

Men, because they have a more dramatic role,
may seem more important to the dance than
women. However, the Ju/'hoansi believe that
men and women make different, but equally
valued, contributions. The singers and dancers
need each others' help to activate the healing
energy. Though the actions of the men and
women at the dance differ, the *n/om* that boils in
them and the resulting experience of *!aia*, or
enhanced awareness, are the same. In the dance,
men and women are as tightly bound together
by their shared experience as they are in their
daily efforts at foraging for the group.

▼ THE PHASES OF A HEALING DANCE ▼

A healing dance is generally held four or five times a month, lasting from dusk to dawn. Most of the community comes to the open center of the camp, where the dance takes place around a fire. The women sit around the flames, shoulder to shoulder, legs intertwined. They sing the healing songs to the beat of their rhythmic clapping while the dancers, who do most of the healing, circle around them. The healers are mostly men, but women sometimes heal as well. At the edges of the open area, others sit around several smaller fires. They support the healing process with their presence, ocassionally singing and dancing.

At the start, the singers and dancers warm up, and the mood is casual and jovial. Many of the dancers are adolescents, showing off new dance steps. Laughter and banter fill the air. Then the mood subtly shifts and grows intense; experienced healers begin to participate. The singing and clapping becomes more spirited and the dancing more focused.

No matter how serious the dance becomes, laughter is never far away. The Ju/'hoansi, unlike many other societies, do not separate worship and everyday life. Although the healing dance is their most spiritual event, they exchange some of their spiciest jokes and tease each other during the ceremony. The dance is an awesome event, but not a solemn one. Even when the mood is

THE FEELING OF N/OM

Tshao, one of the best Ju/'hoansi healers, describes the feeling of n/om in the following way:

"It's a tingling feeling that starts at the base of your spine and works its way up your backbone, until it makes your thoughts become less distinct in your head. Your thoughts begin to swirl and swirl. And the boiling n/om hurts; it is like fire, it burns."

As n/om reaches the base of their skulls, the healers enter an altered state of consciousness called !aia. Once in this state, the dancer can begin to heal.

!Aia, often translated as the word trance, is actually a state of enhanced awareness that gives healers amazing powers to heal. They can travel over great distances in body and mind, see inside other people's bodies, and contact the gods.

most tense, and all are concerned about a dancer overcome with boiling n/om, someone may crack a joke to lighten the atmosphere and give their support.

Toward the middle of the night, in the darkness of the desert, the fire flickers its captivating, pulsating light on the singers and dancers. The feelings run high around the fire and the dancers sweat profusely. When a healer becomes entranced, he or she might begin to stagger, then fall. The healer might shudder and shake violently, his or her whole body convulsing in pain and anguish. Others walk about stiff-legged, their eyes glazed. The state of *!aia* has come, and the healing begins.

The healer who is in *!aia* goes to each person at the dance, whether he or she shows symptoms of illness or not. Healing for the Ju/'hoansi is much more than curing physical or psychological ailments, although it includes that. Healing also means adding to each person's emotional and spiritual growth. All receive the protection of healing. Healers plead and argue with the gods to save a person from illness. They lay their hands on each person and draw out the sickness with eerie shrieks and howls. These cries express the pain and difficulty of the healing work, which may go on for several hours.

As the dance moves into the early morning hours, a calm sets in. Some dancers doze off outside of the dance circle. Others talk quietly and sing softly. Before dawn comes, sleepy figures rise and move toward the dance circle. Once again, the singing becomes strong, the dancing active. There is usually another period of healing as the sun begins to cast its golden light and warmth on the group now huddled around the fire. Before the sun becomes too hot,

the healing usually subsides, the singing slowly softens, then stops. The dance is over.

▼ *!AIA* AND HEALING POWER ▼

The Ju/'hoansi enter *!aia* in order to heal—they do not support anyone who tries to use *!aia* for other purposes. Healing has three main aspects: seeing properly, pulling out the sickness, and arguing with the gods.

When the healers are seeing properly, they can see beyond the surface and into a deeper reality. This special power allows the healer to locate and diagnose the sickness, as well as to begin the actual healing.

Like healers in most other parts of the world, the Ju/'hoansi lay on hands to draw out the sickness. They place their fluttering hands on either side of the person's chest or wherever the sickness is located. They touch the person lightly, or more often vibrate their hands close to the skin's surface. At times healers wrap their bodies around the person being healed, rubbing their sweat—believed to carry healing properties—on the patient. The sickness is drawn into the healers, who then expel the sickness from their own bodies, shaking it from their hands out into space as their bodies shudder with pain.

Ordinarily, the Ju/'hoansi do not speak to the gods. But as the healers work, they not only talk directly to the gods, they may also bargain with,

A BLIND HEALER SEES

Seeing properly enables the healer to see beyond surface appearances to other, deeper realities. Kxao =Oah, an old, blind healer, tells the story of his seeing:

"God keeps my eyeballs in a little cloth bag. When he first took them, he plucked my eyeballs out and put them into the bag. He then tied the eyeballs to his belt and went up to heaven. On the nights that I dance, God comes down from heaven as the singing rises up. He swings the bag with the eyeballs above my head and then lowers the eyeballs to my eye level. As the singing gets strong, he puts the eyeballs back into my sockets. They stay there and I heal. And when the women stop singing and start to disperse, God removes the eyeballs, puts them back in the cloth bag, and takes them up to heaven."

In his daily life, Kxao =Oah cannot see. He walks falteringly and is led about by his wife. But during the dance, he moves gracefully, finding all he needs to touch with his healing hands. In the dance, he sees properly.

insult, or even do battle with them. Healers struggle with the spirits of the dead whom the gods send to carry the sick person away. If a healer's *n/om* is strong, the spirits will retreat and the sick person will be healed and live. This struggle is at the center of the healer's skill, art, and power.

To heal the sick, healers must make contact with spiritual forces. They say that they slip out of their skins and leave their bodies. =Oma Djo, a great healer in Botswana who died in 1995, described the sensation of leaving his body as like that of "breathing, like your breath leaving your mouth." Outside their bodies, the greatest healers say that they climb thin and fragile threads or wires to the sky that lead them to God's village. If the threads break, the fall back to earth is terrifying.

▼ THE STATUS OF HEALERS ▼

Though healers have special psychological qualities, they enjoy no special privileges. Healers, like all Ju/'hoansi, are first hunters and gatherers; only secondarily are they healers.

Yet a few of the most powerful healers are outstanding individuals. For them, daily life is colored by spiritual forces. Some of them dance frequently, sometimes every day; others can heal themselves and others without the support of a full dance. In order to travel faster and further to heal relatives far away, the most distinguished healers can transform themselves into lions.

While the extraordinary power and wisdom of such healers distinguishes them, their social status is equal to that of anyone else in the band. They gain no extra privileges. Healing and spiritual powers are greatly respected, but just as the Ju/'hoansi freely share their food and water, they share their healing energy. Healers, or *n/om kxaosi,* are owners of *n/om*—stewards of that energy. They guide it toward the service of others.

N/om cannot be hoarded; the more it is aroused in one person, the easier it is for someone else to share it. *N/om* expands as it boils and the more it is used for healing, the more it becomes available for further healing. As one healer enters *!aia,* it becomes more likely that another will also.

Boiling *n/om* is likened by the Ju/'hoansi to the sparks that break out in all directions into the dark night when the burning coals in a fire are stirred roughly with a stick. The sparks reach into the far corners of night, touching all in the area with their special light.

Through the healing dance, members of the group stimulate each others' well-being. Each person receives more healing than he or she could possibly derive through individual efforts. The group's healing effort is more than the sum of the individual efforts made.

▼ CONTINUITY AND CHANGE ▼

Archaeological evidence in the Ju/'hoansi area suggests that healing, together with other aspects of Ju/'hoansi life, have been followed by the Ju/'hoansi's ancestors for thousands of years.

Rock paintings on stone surfaces close to ancient camps have many wonderful scenes of

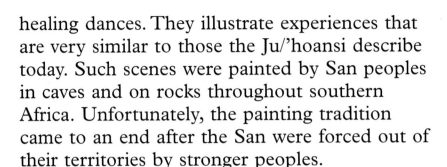

healing dances. They illustrate experiences that are very similar to those the Ju/'hoansi describe today. Such scenes were painted by San peoples in caves and on rocks throughout southern Africa. Unfortunately, the painting tradition came to an end after the San were forced out of their territories by stronger peoples.

Some experts believe that the history of the Ju/'hoansi covers a very long period. Over time, some of the customs and values have changed greatly, yet many have remained the same. In recent years, especially since the late 1960s, San peoples have been forced to confront rapid changes in their way of life. For example, in the late 1970s and 1980s, during the Namibian war of independence, many San were forced to become trackers. Furthermore, they have been encouraged to adopt the Western way of life and become consumers. Many San have lost their land and have had to find new ways to support themselves.

Despite such changes, the San have held fast to their ancient healing dances. It is through continuing their traditions that the San have managed to keep their culture intact through conflicts, changes, and new challenges.▲

chapter

6

A CHANGING ECONOMY

IN THE PAST FEW DECADES THE JU/'HOANSI of Nyae Nyae in Namibia have had to rapidly and creatively adapt to outside pressures. These pressures include the encroachment of cattle herding and mining operations.

Many San groups have adapted by becoming unpaid laborers for cattle-owning societies. In return for their work, they receive milk or meat products, cast-off clothing, and maybe some grain. Without cash, they are trapped in poverty and lose their land. The Namibian Ju/'hoansi have avoided this pattern.

From the 1950s to the 1970s, Namibia, then called South West Africa (SWA), was controlled by the apartheid government of South Africa. The government divided the country into ethnic reservations called homelands. The apartheid government's idea behind the homelands was that black people would be separated from the

The Ju/'hoansi of Nyae Nyae in Namibia have had to adapt to rapid changes in the last few decades. These men and women from Nyae Nyae, wearing Western clothes, are setting out on a joint foraging expedition.

whites. The blacks were forced to move from their lands onto barren scraps of land where few jobs were available.

In 1970 the Ju/'hoansi lost 70 percent of their land. At that time about 2,000 Ju/'hoansi and three families from the Kavango ethnic group had lived in a territory of 18,000 square miles in northeastern Namibia. This land was given to the Kavango as a homeland. Later, another 2,500 square miles became the Kaudum Game Reserve. The Ju/'hoansi were left with about 4,000 square miles of land, enough to support less than 10 percent of their group by hunting and gathering. Over 900 people migrated to settle at the administrative center, Tjum!kui.

The Nyae Nyae Village School Project is one example of how San communities today are taking control of issues that affect them and planning for the future. These four teachers from Nyae Nyae are attending a workshop at Namibia's National Institute for Educational Development.

At Tjum!kui a school, a clinic, a church, a jail, and a store were built, providing work for a few men. Women had little to do, and all the nearby wild food was soon depleted. A large part of the population became dependent on government handouts. Crowding and hunger led to public health problems, enforced idleness led to discontentment, and fighting even broke out after alcohol was introduced. Worse, as the Ju/'hoansi were no longer occupying their land, the government aimed to turn it into a game reserve.

By the late 1970s, the Ju/'hoansi realized that they had to reoccupy their land in order to keep it. Bands were forced to develop strong leaders

51

The Kalahari Desert is a unique and beautiful environment that is of great interest to nature lovers. Today the Ju/'hoansi community is supplementing its income by promoting tourism to the Kalahari.

for the first time. In 1981 three groups returned to their ancestral *n!ores*, or foraging grounds; now there are thirty-five. Since they have much less territory now, they have found ways to supplement their economy, such as herding, wage labor, and tourism.

To support herding and garden projects, the Cattle Fund was formed. This was later transformed into an internationally funded Ju/'hoansi foundation. The foundation helps Ju/'hoansi assert their rights to their land, combat the problems introduced into their society, and make the best use of the land they have left.▲

chapter

7

POLITICS AND
THE FUTURE

IN THE LATE 1970S, THE SOUTH AFRICAN
military in Namibia recruited the San as trackers
for their war against the South West African
People's Organization (SWAPO), which aimed to
liberate the country from oppressive South
African rule. Several hundred Ju/'hoansi took
jobs in the army, not realizing what kind of work
they would be doing. Their relatively large army
salaries created income differences that led to
conflict within their communities. Inexperienced
young Ju/'hoansi soldiers spent their pay on
drink, with chaotic and sometimes violent
results.

In 1986, with the help of the Ju/'hoansi
Foundation, the Ju/wa Farmers Union (JFU) was
formed to deal with the many new problems the
community faced. The JFU represented the *n!ore*
groups from Tjum!kui who had gone back to
their own land. It helped reestablish other

displaced San people according to the old *n!ore* rules. It encouraged new economic strategies and defended the rights of the people against government officials. The JFU reduced a dangerously large lion population, which government officials had encouraged to increase tourism. The JFU also protected water systems from being destroyed by elephants.

Most importantly, the JFU, which later became the Nyae Nyae Farmers Cooperative (NNFC), communicated new understanding and skills and developed a political voice for their community. Many San egalitarian principles easily translated into modern democratic methods.

Today each *n!ore* has two representatives on the Council of the NNFC. Local interests are thus balanced with the goals of the entire community. The NNFC is the guardian of the land and all matters relating to it. New developments are only allowed if they do not threaten the ability of the land to sustain the people. The number of animals is carefully controlled.

The South African military used fear tactics to make the San fight on its side against SWAPO. However, the NNFC worked to inform the San that SWAPO's real aim was to liberate the country according to the United Nations Resolution. Through the Ju/'hoansi foundation, the NNFC helped establish a United Nations presence in Tjum!kui and began to counter the anti-SWAPO

PROPAGANDA

The racist apartheid system was in place in Namibia until 1990 and in South Africa until 1994. It often used negative stereotypes about African peoples to make propaganda (the spread of harmful ideas). The South African army produced a lot of anti-SWAPO propaganda to persuade the San to work as trackers against SWAPO. Crudely drawn leaflets portrayed SWAPO as hyenas chasing the San, who were portrayed as gentle, defenseless antelopes.

When the war ended, SWAPO formed the first independent government of Namibia. Some San feared that their having taken army jobs would count against them in their new country. But Namibia's wise first president, Mr. Sam Nujoma, promised that nobody would be punished for having taken army jobs for economic reasons or for not understanding what the war of liberation had been about. This approach was part of Namibia's general policy of reconciliation, or national peacemaking, designed to heal the wounds of apartheid and war.

After Namibian independence the Ju/'hoansi and other Namibians could see clearly that the propaganda against SWAPO had been totally false. As one of the leaders of the Ju/hoansi said, the propaganda was like the "speech of those who fear greatly."

propaganda spread by the South African military. Soon the community was playing a vital role in liberating themselves and Namibia from apartheid rule.

In 1990, during the elections for an independent Namibia, a large proportion of the Ju/'hoansi population turned out as informed voters. In a few short years, their community had faced terrible challenges with courage and intelligence and adapted with remarkable flexibility. The consciousness of the Ju/'hoansi had been changed forever. They had discovered that their own efforts could make a difference on the national level.

Their growing political awareness helped the Ju/'hoansi build their economy. With the help of the NNFC and their Foundation, the people of Nyae Nyae drilled wells, built kraals (corrals) for small cattle herds, and started dryland gardens and some small irrigated gardens. They also began selling their handicrafts and made plans for community

This beautiful leather skirt is decorated with ostrich eggshell beads. The San use ostrich eggs to carry precious water. If the eggs break, shell fragments are formed into small round disks by scraping them on a stone. The disks are strung together into strands. Today the San often use imported glass beads.

stewardship of natural resources. Some of these activities were not allowed during the apartheid government's rule. The new Namibian government has encouraged the Ju/'hoansi community to become self-sufficient.

The language of the Ju/'hoansi was first written down at the time of Namibian independence. Under the new Namibian constitution, the Ju/'hoansi and other Namibians have the right to be educated in their own language and to use it in all dealings with the national government. This guarantees that they can express themselves effectively and that

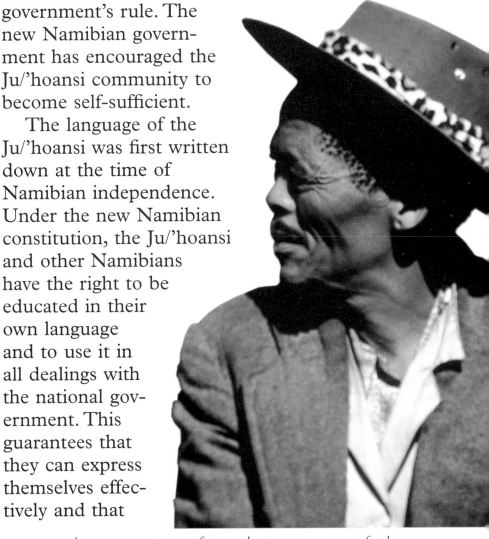

Seen above is !Xuma/Kunta from Dobe in Botswana. A gifted translator, language teacher, and storyteller, he has played an important role in passing on San traditions and teaching them to others. Megan Biesele, coauthor of this book, first learned to speak the language of the Ju/'hoansi from !Xuma/Kunta twenty-five years ago, when this picture was taken.

Today the Ju/'hoansi are part of the independent country of Namibia. They play an active role in determining the future direction of their community. This young man, wearing a tufted hairstyle popular among his age group, is free to decide how best to adapt the ancient traditions of his people to new challenges.

their language will be preserved. The survival of their language is intimately connected to the survival of their culture as a whole.

One year after independence, which Ju/'hoansi celebrated by dancing in the streets with other Namibians, they raised their newfound political voice at the Namibian National Conference on Land Reform and the Land Question. NNFC leaders argued brilliantly for the *n!ore* system of land stewardship to receive special recognition in Namibia. Speaking in their own language through translators and with the aid of documents and

Today the NNFC plays a leading role in Ju/'hoansi affairs and their relationship to the outside world. Seen above is Kxao =Oma, the current manager of the NNFC who has also played a leading role in beginning education projects in his community. He uses this beach ball with a map of the world to give children in the village a sense of their place in the world.

graphics, they asked that their ancient traditions form a basis for decisions about land in their area. They have won a first round in this right to self-determination, laying the foundations for a future that they can map out according to their egalitarian and ecologically sound principles.

As part of the large country of Namibia, which consists of many different communities and cultures, the Ju/'hoansi do not see their effort as isolated, but rather as part of a larger picture. As a chairperson of the Nyae Nyae Farmers Cooperative sums it up:

The San are famous for the beautiful rock art that they painted and engraved throughout much of southern Africa. The San have not continued these rock art traditions, but some San artists are now making modern paintings on paper and canvas.

"We Ju/'hoansi feel that different people, like different communities, have different strengths, and that the only thing that works is using our different strengths together."▲

60

Glossary

affluent Wealthy.

!aia A state of heightened awareness and strength, developed during the healing dance.

apartheid Government system based on controlling people by keeping them in separate racial groups.

deities Lesser gods that are believed to control different aspects of life.

egalitarianism The principle that people should be equal in terms of wealth and status.

foraging Living by hunting and gathering wild foods.

indigenous Something (people, plants, animals, etc.) that occurs naturally in a particular region or environment.

kxaosi Owners; persons with expert knowledge of a resource who make decisions on how to best share the resource.

n!ao The positive energy shared by newborn babies, hunted animals, and the weather.

n!om A spiritual force or energy used in healing.

n!ore A hunting and gathering territory.

social stratification To divide into classes based on wealth or status.

stereotype A generalized view of another group of people.

For Further Reading

Barnard, Alan. *Kalahari Bushmen*. New York: Thomson Learning, 1993.

Lewis-Williams, J. D. *Discovering Southern African Rock Art*. Cape Town, South Africa: David Philip, 1990.

Thomas, E. *The Harmless People*. New York: Knopf, 1959.

Challenging Reading

Barnard, A. *Hunters and Herders of Southern Africa: A Comparative Ethnography of the Khoisan Peoples*. Cambridge, England: Cambridge University Press, 1992.

Biesele, M. *"Women Like Meat": The Folklore and Foraging Ideology of the Kalahari Ju/'hoan*. Bloomington: Indiana University Press, 1993.

Katz, R., M. Biesele, and V. St. Denis. *"Healing Makes Our Hearts Happy": Spirituality and Transformation Among the Ju/'hoansi of the Kalahari*. Rochester, VT: Inner Traditions International, 1997.

Lee, R. *The Dobe Ju/'hoansi*. Second ed. Fort Worth: Harcourt, Brace, 1993.

Marshall, L. *The !Kung of Nyae Nyae*. Cambridge, MA: Harvard University Press, 1976.

Index

ACKNOWLEDGMENTS

The author would very much like to thank the Ju/'hoansi people at the Nyae Nyae Farmers Cooperative; Lesley Beake, author of *The Song of Be*, for suggesting age-appropriate language for this book; Richard Katz for materials on Ju/'hoansi healing; the late Patrick Dickens for his orthographic work among Ju/'hoansi; and the late Marjorie Shostak, author of *Nisa*, for bringing authentic Ju/'hoansi voices to world attention.

ABOUT THE AUTHORS

Megan Biesele is an anthropologist who has lived with the Ju/'hoansi for almost ten years. Kxao Royal /O/oo has played a historic role as one of the first two English-speaking San schoolteachers employed by the Namibian Ministry of Education. The authors first met in Botswana in the 1970s. They have worked closely together on several translation projects, including the Ju/'hoansi statements for the Namibian National Land Conference in 1991.

PHOTO CREDITS

Cover, pp. 18 (top and middle), 25 (bottom), 33 (top), 50, 51, 52, 57 © Megan Biesele; pp. 8, 58 © Dee Worman; pp. 33 (bottom), 34 courtesy of the Department of Wildlife and National Parks, Botswana; p. 56 photo by Michael Hall, courtesy of the University of the Witwatersrand Art Galleries; pp. 15, 20 by R. K. Hitchcock; p. 18 (bottom) by S. Barclay; p. 21 by C. Ritchie; pp. 25 (top), 26, 39, 40 by K. and C. Brown; pp. 31, 59 by M. Heckler; p. 60 (all four images) by B. and R. Clauss.

CONSULTING EDITOR

Gary N. van Wyk, Ph.D.

LAYOUT AND DESIGN

Kim Sonsky